For Tara, Dez, & Dash,
my partners in exploration.

— JCT

For my parents and my sisters.

— PK

Special thanks to Richard Brunning for his amazing

feedback and help on the layout.

Yuri stood on the launchpad.

He looked at his rocket.

He was very scared.

He was very excited.

Yuri was very brave.

Earth is big.
It holds us to the ground.

But Yuri's rocket was strong.

It would lift him up into outer space.

It was time to leave Earth.

Yuri's friends said goodbye.

He climbed inside the rocket.

Yuri pushed buttons.

He waited for the signal.

He pushed the last button.

The big rocket rumbled around Yuri.

The rocket shot fire from its engines.

He said, "Let's go!"

The rocket pushed Yuri up slowly,

then faster,

and faster.

Yuri went higher than a bird,

higher than a cloud,

higher than an airplane.

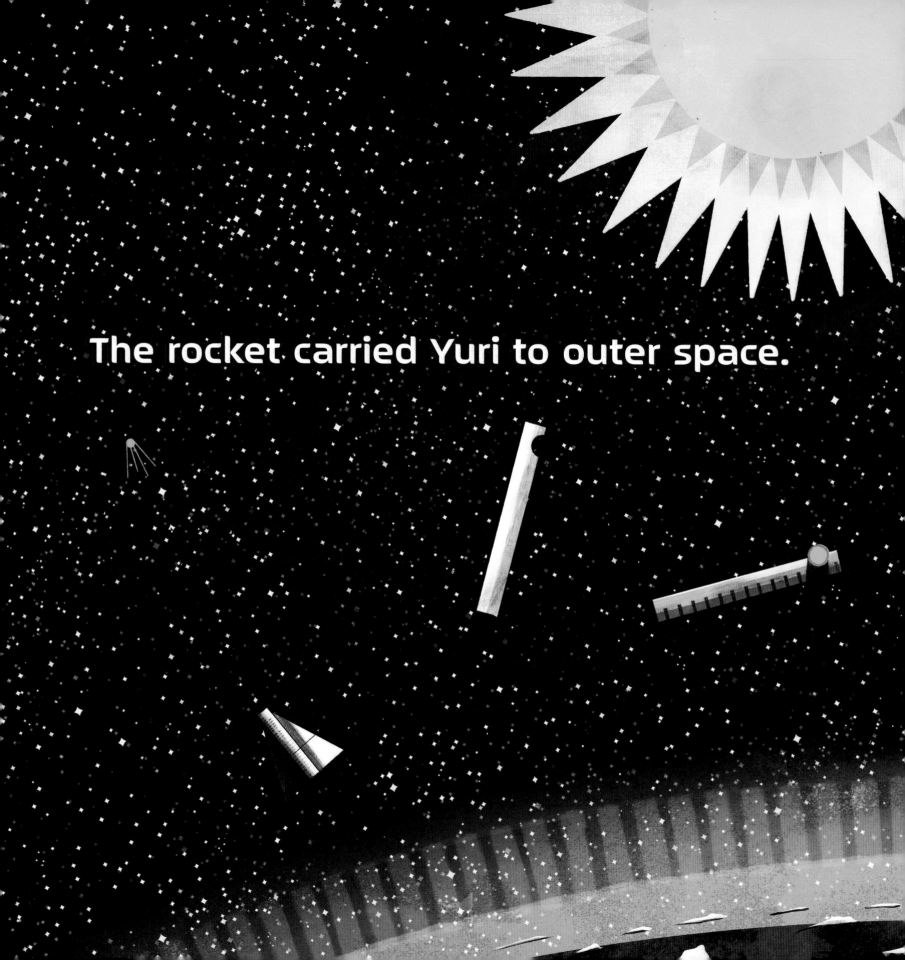

The rocket carried Yuri to outer space.

There is no air to breathe in space,
and it is very cold.

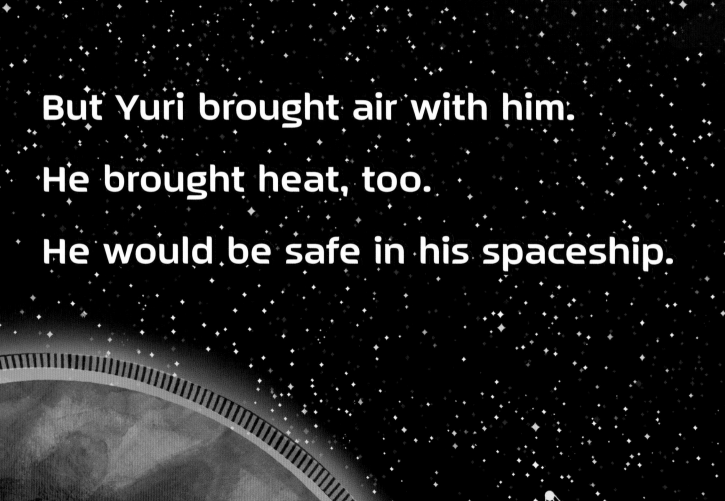

But Yuri brought air with him.

He brought heat, too.

He would be safe in his spaceship.

Out of the tiny spaceship window,

Yuri looked down at Earth.

The Earth was so beautiful.

Yuri was on the
other side of the sky.

It was delicate and blue from above.

It turned to purple where day met night.

Yuri saw a rainbow,

from the ground into the sky.

He said, "Such a rainbow!"

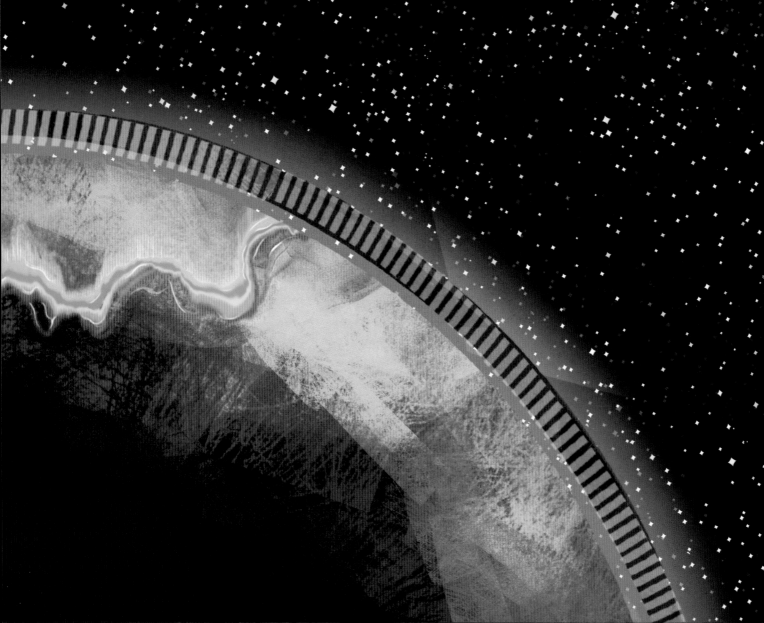

Yuri's spaceship turned

toward outer space.

He could see so many stars in the black.

He said, "A very pretty sight."

And then

came the Sun!

Our star, so bright,

Yuri could see nothing else.

He said,

"The Sun is running the solar system."

Now, it was time to leave space.

Yuri left his spaceship.

Time to go back to Earth.

Yuri's adventure was almost over.

He parachuted to the ground.

He was very scared.

He was very excited.

Yuri's friends were waiting for him.

They were all very happy.

They wanted to hear about Yuri's trip.

Yuri had left the Earth.

Yuri had been the first.

For Parents' Eyes ONLY!

Yuri Alekseyevich Gagarin (March 9, 1934 — March 27, 1968) became the first person launched into outer space on April 12, 1961. He was a citizen of the Union of Soviet Socialist Republics (USSR). His 108-minute flight consisted of a single orbit in his Vostok 3KA spacecraft, launched from the Baikonur Cosmodrome.

Yuri skimmed the upper atmosphere at around 169 kilometers above the Earth's surface.

During his flight, he reported seeing many remarkable things, including a rainbow on Earth, stars, and the sun.

After the orbit, Yuri's craft descended to about 7 kilometers above earth, where he ejected from the Vostok and parachuted the rest of the way to the ground. Technically, this invalidated his record since, according to international rules, the first space flight required that the pilot land with the craft, so the Soviet Union insisted that he landed with the Vostok, despite evidence to the contrary.

No one questions his accomplishment today.

Celebrate Yuri's Night!

Yuri's Night is a global celebration of humanity's past, present, and future in space. Yuri's Night parties and events are held around the world every April in commemoration of Yuri Gagarin becoming the first human to venture into space in 1961, and the inaugural launch of the first Space Shuttle in 1981.

Join parties around the world celebrating Yuri Gagarin's first flight, and the future of space flight every April 12th!

Yuri's Night events combine space-themed fun with education and outreach. These events can range from an all-night mix of techno and technology at a NASA Center, to a movie showing and stargazing at your local museum or science center, to a gathering of friends at your school or home.

Find a party near you or start one of your own at

www.yurisnight.net

Thanks to...

Ada and Ivor

Aleena S. Narithookil

Alex Huffaker

Boyd Davis

Carmen Gloria

Chris Boese

Corey & Ashley Lafferty

Daniel Hoy

Desmond and Rowan

Ramesh and
Devyani Kodavatiganti

Eloise & Olivia

Gowri Reddy

Gracie and Laurie Fox

Greg Nudelman

Isabel Miranda

Jared L

Jay Moore

Jeff Newelt

Jotica

Kellan and Parker Jones

Kyle McCabe

Lakshmi & Lakshman

Margret

Matt Blum

Matthew Fisher

Milo Thomas

Nancy

Owen Thomas

Phillip Djwa

Phoenix Hull

Raja Schaar

Rekha Mallela

Richard Bruning

Rohan Gowda

Santos Irvine

Sarah Preston

Sarmad and Yara Jabri

Sophia

Steffen Jauch

Stuart Robson

Susie King Taylor Community School
in Savannah, GA

The Arvind Jain and Family

The Bailey Family

The Furniss Family

The Kodavatiganti Family

The Maheshwari Family

The Popkin family

The Pushkala Iyer and Family

The Rekha Mallela and Family

The Tushar Jain and Family

Yuri Linaschke

...Whose support made this book possible.